Original title:

What Happens When Life Doesn't Make Sense

Author: Seraphina Caldwell

ISBN HARDBACK: 978-1-80566-156-6

ISBN PAPERBACK: 978-1-80566-451-2

The Language of Unspoken Turmoil

A chicken crossed, to where, who knows,
While pondering life's quirky woes.
With eggs that debate the sunny side,
And socks that refuse to abide.

The cat is plotting, or so they say,
While mice dance like it's their grand ballet.
In cereal boxes, secrets reside,
Like lost keys playing hide-and-seek wide.

Beneath the Weight of Silence

A lizard tap dances on the wall,
While schmeering peanut butter on the call.
Gum stuck in hair, a fashion faux pas,
And no one quite fits in this bizarre bazaar.

The toaster burns bread to a crisp,
While spoons conspire to do a wisp.
In the land of lost socks and odd tape,
Even whispers are dressed in a cape.

The Chronology of Chaos

A calendar misplaced its days,
Fruity loops giggle in maze-like ways.
Time trips over its untied shoe,
While shovels shout, 'We're overdue!'

In a land where clocks slurp jellybeans,
Waffles reign with syrupy dreams.
With convoluted paths to where we walk,
Seeing blue elephants quietly talk.

Mismatched Shoes on a Winding Path

One shoe sings, and the other just sighs,
As they wander under cotton candy skies.
Rabbits juggle carrots in the mix,
While pancakes ponder tricky politics.

A hiccup in logic, a wink from a tree,
Confetti bursts forth, just wait and see.
In a world where smoothies have no end,
And craziness is a quirky friend.

The Portrait of the Unpredictable

In a world where socks don't match,
And traffic lights play hide and seek,
I order fish but get a hat,
Life's a riddle, quite unique.

A cat that thinks it's a dog,
Sings opera under the full moon,
Spaghetti grows upon the trees,
And pancakes dance to a cartoon.

We wear our shoes upon our heads,
And chase the clouds on sunny days,
Through markets where the pickles jog,
And lemons ride on purple rays.

So raise a toast to all the quirks,
To every giggle and wild surprise,
For life's a circus made for laughs,
With rainbows sprouting in the skies.

The Desert of Confusion

In a land where cacti wear shoes,
I ponder the meaning of my morning snooze.
The sun's hot, but so is my plan,
To find why a penguin can't drive a van.

A mirage tells me to take a leap,
But all that glitters is lost in sleep.
Lizards laugh, they know the score,
While I chase my thoughts behind closed doors.

Each grain of sand has a riddle to tell,
Like why my socks don't match so well.
I trip on air, then I trip on time,
Is there a punchline buried in this rhyme?

Yet in this dry, absurd expanse,
I dance with shadows in a silly prance.
For all this chaos may seem like a mess,
I find the joy in the big, fat guess.

Reflections in a Distorted Mirror

I look in the glass, and what do I see?
A chicken in shades, cranking up the O.C.
My hair's a toupee, my nose is too long,
As I ponder the wisdom of singing a song.

The mirror winks back with a silly grin,
It knows I'm not tuned to the proper spin.
A reflection of donuts, my thoughts in a whirl,
As I visualize life as a cereal swirl.

If horse shoes are lucky, what's a shoe with a cat?
Does it make me the ruler of all things spat?
With a giggle and wiggle, I strut, I preen,
In a world that's absurd, I'm the queen of the scene.

So let's raise a toast to the things that confuse,
Life's a funhouse, and we're all welcome to cruise.
Each twist and turn might leave us in stitches,
But I'll take the laughter, for that's what enriches.

A Kaleidoscope of Uncertainty

Through the lens of my glass, things twist and shake,
A cat wearing a hat throws a cake in the lake.
Colors collide in a vibrant display,
While I ponder if cheese can ever fly away.

The world flips around like a topsy-turvy ride,
And I find myself laughing, with no place to hide.
With each turn I find a fish on a bike,
Is it strange? Perhaps, but so is my type.

I count the jellybeans, that rainbow parade,
As I question if clouds can ever be made.
Why does the sun like to snooze at noon?
While a bear in a bowtie plays old-time tunes.

Yet in this whirlwind of bright, silly dreams,
I dance with the shadows, or that's how it seems.
For in this lightshow of wacky delight,
Life's chaos just feels wonderfully right.

Uncharted Waters of the Mind

I sailed on a boat made of rubber and cheese,
With a crew of old socks that always say 'please.'
The waves are like marshmallows, fluffy and white,
While I navigate dreams in a whimsical flight.

The compass spins wild, with no sense of care,
As I fish for ideas from the cool ocean air.
An octopus offers to teach me to dance,
While seagulls critique my unique style of prance.

I dive through the depths of a chocolate sea,
In search of the jelly that's hiding from me.
Fish in bow ties recite Shakespeare on cue,
As I ponder the wisdom of what's really true.

Though the currents may swirl and the tides may
confound,
I savor the laughter in the chaos I've found.
For in these uncharted, perplexing waves,
I find that the joy is in the foolhardy braves.

The Silent Jumble

In a room full of shoes, a cat takes a stroll,
Frog in a tuxedo, chasing a roll.
Whispers of pancakes float through the air,
While broccoli dances, free without care.

An owl wears a hat, big glasses askew,
And the toaster sings songs about cheese fondue.
Butterflies argue with a globe made of pie,
As rainbows plot mischief in the sky.

A shoe with a sock claims it's the queen,
While spaghetti confetti fills in between.
And a bear pulls a boat through a pool made of dreams,
Just to test if it floats, or so it seems.

So when logic escapes on a wild midnight ride,
Just laugh with the nonsense, let humor collide.
For life's just a puzzle with pieces askew,
And the best kind of laughter is always brand new.

Dancing with Confusion

A penguin in boots does the cha-cha around,
With spaghetti and meatballs all tangled and browned.
Chickens in sequin have taken the floor,
While a cactus in dance shoes keeps asking for more.

The clock sings a tune, time runs in retreat,
As jellybeans giggle and take to the street.
A giraffe in a tutu does pirouettes tall,
While the fish in the pond have a glitterball.

Mice race on tricycles, hats on their heads,
As cupcakes bounce lightly on soft, fluffy beds.
Why not embrace this chaotic ballet,
With each silly step, let your worries decay?

So twirl with the madness, let laughter ignite,
In this zany circus, everything's bright.
For when life's a conundrum, just dance like a fool,
And trust that confusion can sometimes be cool.

A Maze of Half-Truths

At the end of a rainbow, I found a lost shoe,
Worn by a dragon that's plotting a coup.
Marshmallows whisper of secrets untold,
While a wizard counts jellybeans, brave and bold.

In a forest of noodles, where noodles like trees,
Birds wear top hats and converse with the bees.
Fish ride bicycles, and the sun just spins,
As laughter erupts from the tuba's own grins.

The moon plays chess with a butterfly knight,
While clouds clink their glasses, involving delight.
Pirates who treasure a map made of cheese,
Seek out the fortune in ticklish breeze.

Amidst all these riddles, with giggles galore,
The truth's just a jester, always wanting more.
So let's dive in the maze, let the fun be the key,
For the quirkiest journeys bring lighthearted glee.

When Shadows Speak in Tongues

In shadows that shuffle, whispers are found,
They talk of old socks that go round and round.
A rhino in pajamas, snoring like thunder,
While ants weave a tapestry, full of wonder.

With giggles and grumbles, the shadows conspire,
To bake a big pie, made of mud and of fire.
They argue in riddles, and frolic with flair,
As the toaster commands them to dance in midair.

A shadow in glasses claims it can see,
All the wishes that float on the edges of glee.
A puppy debates with a pumpkin on dreams,
In a world where nothing is quite what it seems.

So listen for laughter in darkened embrace,
For shadows may chatter while they jiggle in place.
In the oddness of life, where giggles arise,
The funniest stories unfold from the wise.

The Question Without an Answer

Why do socks always disappear,
While my laundry sings in cheer?
I ponder, scratch my puzzled head,
As laundry gremlins dance instead.

Is it the dryer or a ghost?
Or just the socks that love to boast?
They frolic free, no need to wear,
Leaving me searching everywhere.

The toaster burns my toast in rage,
While I flip through the fridge's page.
My lunch escapes, but where's the fun?
Oh, that lunch must be on the run!

And yet I laugh in puzzling flight,
For life is strange, but that feels right.
In chaos, there's a hidden plan,
Like socks and toast, we'll understand!

Shadows in the Twilight

The cat's convinced she's part of art,
Napping on my laptop, oh so smart.
I work and squint through feline bliss,
As she dreams deep, won't take a miss.

The clock ticks weird, it jumps and skips,
My coffee spills, oh sweet eclipse.
As shadows play a game of tag,
I look for answers in this rag.

A doorbell rings, but who's that there?
A pizza? Or a ghost in my chair?
I fumble keys like jumbled jokes,
And laugh at life's enchanted hoax.

Yet as the twilight spins its web,
I find a smile on what's misled.
In silly mixes, truth may lie,
Just dance along, don't ask me why!

Where Solitude Meets Confusion

In my solitude, I trip on air,
A dance of socks with no one there.
The walls replay my laugh aloud,
Echoing thoughts that feel too proud.

I juggle fruit, or so I try,
But apples roll and oranges fly.
In kitchen chaos, plans go out,
Where did my sanity scout about?

The fridge hums tunes of mystery,
While I'm locked in grocery history.
Who knew the pickles loved to chat,
While I just search for my lost hat?

But in this riddle, strange yet bright,
Laughter's spark ignites the night.
In tangled threads of musing bliss,
Jokes in confusion, I can't miss!

Threads of Uncertainty

My shoelaces tie themselves in knots,
While I chase thoughts that roam in spots.
The world spins round in dizzy spree,
As socks and dreams collide with glee.

The dishes dance like they're alive,
While I wonder where the spoons derive.
Why do meetings turn to jest?
At least the coffee works its best!

I plant a seed to grow a tree,
But all I get is mystery.
A garden of beans turns into peas,
Just add some laughter, if you please!

In threads of life, a fabric spun,
Each twist reveals a part of fun.
As confusions thread through every day,
I find the humor in the fray!

Where Certainty Fades

In a world where socks disappear,
The fabric of logic wears thin.
I search for my mind in the fridge,
Yet all I find is a grin.

Kittens dance on the ceiling fan,
While numbers do the cha-cha real fast.
I ponder the fate of my lunch,
Did it really think it could last?

The coffee spills secrets to the wall,
As the clock decides not to tick.
Life's riddles wrapped in bubble wrap,
And my sanity can't find the trick.

So I wear mismatched shoes today,
And take laughter as my guide.
In this carnival of confusion,
Who'd want to take a ride?

Metaphors for Disarray

A fish in a tree quite surprised,
As gravity takes a break.
Peanut butter hugs my goldfish,
While he dreams of a steak.

Butterflies recite Shakespeare,
To the tune of a heavy bass.
The cactus wears a tutu now,
As I join the wild chase.

Where do the biscuits go at night?
With magic wands and twinkling eyes?
I tripped on a cloud this morning,
And fell to my donut surprise.

So I scribble my thoughts on napkins,
And toast to the abstract sounds.
In this circus of metaphors,
The punchline's lost, but joy abounds.

The Space Between Reason

Here in the space where logic bends,
I ask, 'Is this a taco or cat?'
A penguin steals my sandwich,
As I frown and adjust my hat.

The microwave whispers to me,
"Your leftovers wear a crown."
I ponder the wisdom of the chair,
While the ceiling jokes around.

Why does the cereal float away?
I swear it danced with the moon.
A toaster sings an opera,
Leaving me in a happy swoon.

So I embrace the nonsense, my friend,
With a wiggle and a wink.
Life's best when it breaks the mold,
And turns every thought to pink.

Shattered Reflections

In shards of glass, a vision laughs,
A puzzle missing its pieces.
The chicken crossed into my thoughts,
As my logic slowly ceases.

Eyebrows dance upon my face,
Like they're starring in a play.
I wear my pants inside-out,
And call it Fashion Day.

The moon's a cheese wheel spinning fast,
While rainbows paint the ground.
I shared my secrets with a fox,
Who said nothing can be found.

So grab your shoes and tiptoe light,
Through the laughter and the mess.
When life tips over, just roll with it,
For chaos wears a funny dress.

A Mind in Flux

Thoughts take a jog, then a dance,
Lost in a shuffle, not a chance.
A sock on my foot, another in hand,
How did my morning get so unplanned?

Statements bubble, float like balloons,
Nonsense spills out, like runaway tunes.
My coffee tastes like a dance on a grill,
Is that my heart racing, or just the thrill?

The clock on the wall is playing a game,
It's mocking my life, with no hint of shame.
Time's taking a stroll, it's out for a spin,
While I search for a reason I can fit in.

So I laugh at the chaos, absurdity reigns,
As logic forgets all its personal gains.
Life's a circus, it teeters and sways,
I'll grab a popcorn, and enjoy the crazed.

The Incoherent Symphony

A kazoo quite absurd plays in my brain,
With trombones that wobble, creating the pain.
Flutes make decisions that go to the moon,
While the drums keep a beat, like a cat in a swoon.

Instruments clash, it's a cacophony fine,
What key are we in? Is it wry or divine?
Concerts of chaos on repeat in my head,
Even the violins drop notes, hearty and red.

The conductor was late, or maybe just lost,
He's sipping hot tea, what a curious cost.
The audience laughs, in this ruckus they find,
That life's wild anthem is a comedy kind.

So let's orchestrate mayhem, it's music for fools,
With sounds like my thoughts, breaking all of the rules.
In laughter, we'll find a sweet symphonic blend,
Where nonsense and joy come together as friends.

Flickers of Dissonance

Lightning bugs buzzing in a sock drawer,
Why is the cat trying to open the door?
Fridge magnets whisper in a language unknown,
While the toaster just popped out a half-eaten scone.

Clouds wear silly hats made of mashed potatoes,
Underneath unicorns in funky shoes stratos.
I check my shoes—am I wearing two lefts?
Or is that just life, playing with thefts?

With every tick-tock, my thoughts flip and whirl,
Dancing with crayons on a merry-go-girl.
Reality giggles, sheds a sneaky grin,
As I trip on a dream, and then start to spin.

So here's to the odd, the cracked and the chipped,
Life's a slapstick routine, come watch it unzipped.
Chaos is laughter, it's bright and profound,
In dissonant flickers, pure joy can be found.

The Riddle of Existence

A turtle in a top hat asks me for change,
While ducks in a row look positively strange.
Why does my cereal taste like a shoe?
Is that a banana, or just peek-a-boo?

The sun wears sunglasses, too bright for the day,
And clouds have opinions, but who should I say?
I search for my keys in the fridge, oh so smart,
But instead find a pickle, now that's quite the art.

Lost in a puzzle with pieces that fit,
But one of them vanished, it's part of the skit.
Life's riddles are giggles that lead me astray,
While socks make a run for freedom, hooray!

So here's to the questions that lead me in loops,
While I munch on my dreams and hang out with owls,
woo-hoos.
It's all quite absurd, not a stitch out of place,
In this riddle of existence, silliness takes grace.

Beyond the Horizon of Understanding

I tried to bake a cake one day,
But used salt instead of sugar, hooray!
The frosting ran like a salty stream,
And left me questioning my wild dream.

A fish wore shoes and danced a jig,
While I cracked jokes that fell too big.
The cat looked on in utter glee,
As logic slipped right past the key.

A squirrel held court with a wise old goat,
Discussing life while wearing a coat.
I took notes on their comical plight,
Then lost my pen—oh what a sight!

Sometimes all that makes sense is the mess,
These moments create a chuckle, I confess.
Beyond the horizon, things may seem bright,
But I'll take my giggles in the dead of night.

Vestiges of a Confounded Heart

I asked the moon for a pinch of wisdom,
And got a wink as an exquisite rhythm.
A cactus wore a hat at the fair,
While I tripped on clouds without a care.

Thoughts in my head just danced around,
Like squirrels at play in my backyard bound.
The toaster gave a speech, so quite refined,
But all I wanted was my toast well-defined.

A backward clock rang at half-past three,
And I pondered what it all meant to me.
The tree tried to gossip with passing breeze,
While I scrabbled to catch thoughts as they tease.

Confused but chuckling, I embraced the charm,
In a world turned around, I faced no harm.
Every laugh echoed the quirks of the heart,
In these vestiges, I found my art.

The Storm We Never Named

Raindrops fell like jelly beans,
Each splash igniting silly dreams.
The clouds were made of cotton candy,
And I felt my thoughts become quite dandy.

Umbrellas turned to wild balloons,
As people danced to the song of loons.
A fish in a top hat said, 'Good day!'
While I stood by laughing at the play.

Puddles mirrored my curious glances,
Reflecting moments of oddball chances.
On rubber boots, I took a leap,
As laughter bubbled and memories steeped.

In every downpour, joy was found,
Though sanity seemed to float around.
I ran through chaos, embraced the game,
In the storm we never named, who's to blame?

Short Stories of the Unseen

I once met a ghost with a taste for cheese,
He'd tell me tales of the wind and leaves.
Butterflies debated their favorite hue,
While I pondered what I thought I knew.

A rabbit wore glasses and read the news,
While squirrels debated the best kind of shoes.
The invisible cat just purred with delight,
While I scribbled down nonsense late into the night.

Dreams once tangled like a ball of yarn,
Came unwound in a cosmic barn.
With each stitch of absurdity, I found,
Short stories of unseen joy abound.

So here's to moments that puzzle the mind,
Where laughter and chaos are perfectly aligned.
In this quirky tapestry, I weave my view,
With threads of delight in each silly hue.

Unraveled Threads of Thought

In a world where ducks wear hats,
And cats speak in riddles, oh so sprat,
My cereal dances, my toast takes flight,
I ponder the meaning of left and right.

The sun plays hide and seek with the moon,
While vegetables hum a silly tune,
My socks plot mischief, oh what a sight,
As I chase my thoughts into the night.

Jellybeans score points in a basketball game,
And pickles rejoice when I yell their name,
Life's quirky puzzle, a jumbled spree,
Where logic retreats, leaving only glee.

With each twist and turn, I laugh and I play,
As coffee spills beans on this bewildering day,
Threads unraveling, yet here's the core,
It's all just a game, who could ask for more?

In the Eye of the Storm

Riding a whirlwind on a pink flamingo,
While clouds throw confetti in a wild tango,
I trip on rainbows, slip on the breeze,
Finding my balance with a sneeze and a wheeze.

The ducks are debating over chess with a fox,
As ninjas in pajamas throw popcorn at clocks,
Each tick-tock is bouncy, elastic like gum,
And unicorns giggle while I twist and hum.

In the center of chaos, there's such a delight,
A spotlight on penguins that dance through the night,
The storm may be wild, but I can't help but grin,
For life's a circus, a whimsical spin.

With pies in the sky and clouds made of cream,
I laugh at the nonsense, as wild as it seems,
Each moment's a puzzle, each giggle a gem,
In this eye of the storm, I find my zen.

Hidden Patterns in the Chaos

In the jumbled mess of everyday quirks,
I find hidden patterns in slippery jerks,
The cat's wearing glasses, the dog's on a call,
As chaos unfolds, I just ponder it all.

Spaghetti's dancing with meatballs so bold,
While shadows recite mysteries untold,
The walls whisper secrets of tales gone awry,
As I sip on my juice with a side of pie.

A circus of flavors, each meal a surprise,
As pickles and cupcakes go after the prize,
I follow the laughter through thick and through thin,
Who knew that confusion could be such a win?

Among tangled tripwires of life's crazy thread,
I juggle the nonsense and plenty of bread,
In chaos, I see, life's a comedic show,
With laughter as currency, I'm rich, don't you know?

When Time Stands Still

Time stood still, or so it might seem,
As I chase a snail in a wobbly dream,
Clocks spin in circles, while turtles shout, "Go!"
A dance of confusion, a whimsical show.

The ice cream melts faster than thoughts slip away,
While socks hold court on this curious day,
With jellybeans forming a council of glee,
And penguins in bowties all yelling, "Yippee!"

As funny as fortune when laughter prevails,
I ride on the back of a kite, sans sails,
With balloon animals helping me steer,
In a timeless zone of hysterics and cheer.

So let's toast to hours that dance in the breeze,
With nonsense galore, and currants on trees,
When time stands still, I've discovered it's true,
That silliness reigns in this wild rendezvous.

The Misplaced Clock

A clock that ticks but runs awry,
Its hands dance like a drunken fly.
Breakfast at night, and lunch at dawn,
Time's a jester, laughing on.

The seconds leap like rabbits wild,
"Make haste!" they shout, "We're all beguiled!"
Yet here I sit, not knowing when,
Is it noon or time for zen?

I try to follow its silly tune,
But missed my train, oh what a croon!
With every tick, my plans take flight,
And sleep becomes a game tonight.

Oh, misplaced clock, what snickers you weave,
You turn my day to a sitcom reprieve!
I'll dance with time, in playful chat,
As hours laugh and tell me "spat!"

Tangled in Eclipses

In a world where shadows cheer and play,
The sun forgot to shine today.
I tripped on clouds adorned in socks,
And giggled at the tangled clocks.

Eclipses grin with crooked beams,
They write my fate in silly dreams.
Lost in a maze of light and shade,
I question why my logic's frayed.

With every twist, a prank unfolds,
As laughter drowns the tale it molds.
The stars conspire with gleeful glitz,
And I just dance with zany fits.

Oh cosmos bright, you fickle friend,
Your jokes may baffle, yet never end.
In tangled rays, I find delight,
As silliness grows bright in night.

The Broken Compass

A compass spins, but never points,
It wanders on, to tease and taunt.
"North? South? Who cares!" it seems to say,
As I meander through disarray.

With a chuckle, I follow the breeze,
Turning left while my mind disagrees.
Mountains turn into silly hills,
As laughter echoes, chasing thrills.

Each step a step into the unknown,
As mushrooms dance on circles grown.
A pathway smiles, then rolls away,
And trees wink at me in their own ballet.

Oh broken compass, lead me astray,
In your quirky game, I'll laugh and sway.
For when directions simply furl,
Adventure spins a dizzy whirl.

Between Truth and Illusion

In a land where reality slips and slides,
A penguin shops for jellybeans and rides.
Truth in a tutu, dancing on air,
While muffins gossip, unaware.

I asked a rabbit by a pie stand,
"Is this the truth or a strange brand?"
He winked and said, "Why not both?"
As I pondered my sense-keeping oath.

Illusions leap like frogs on a line,
Making friendships with marshmallow wine.
As every question spins and flips,
I chuckled at the world's silly quips.

Between the lines of nonsense drawn,
A giggle blooms like a floral dawn.
So let's embrace this wobbly dance,
In truth and illusion, let's take a chance!

Where the Stars Don't Align

The cat wore a hat, that's quite rare,
Dancing on tables, without a care.
Socks mismatched, both red and blue,
Is this a party, or a zoo?

Pickles on ice cream, what a treat,
The toast's doing yoga, quite hard to beat.
A toaster's opinion on life's great plan,
I guess it's all part of the master plan.

A fish in a car, so chic and sleek,
It rolls down the street, no one would speak.
A banana slides by, quite surprised,
In a world like this, who's realized?

So laugh at the chaos, embrace the odd,
For life's a giggle, let's give a nod.
With silly things swirling all around,
In the stretch of logic, joy is found.

The Unraveled Narrative

Once upon a time, or so they say,
A frog wore a crown, on a Thursday.
The princess ignored him, far too busy,
With a dance-off, it's really quite dizzy.

The owls in tuxedos kept score,
While squirrels debated the age of the door.
A sandwich union began to protest,
Demanding all jelly be put to the test.

Balloons floating high, quite confused,
Wondering why confetti got snoozed.
The king's jester tripped, fell on a pie,
Never knew laughter would make him cry.

And so the tale twirls, round and round,
In the realm of the silly, joy is found.
With every quirk adding to the plot,
Life laughs at itself, forgetting what's not.

Seeking Clarity in the Fog

Through a foggy morning, I stumbled blind,
Chased by a duck, what a rare kind.
It quacked with purpose, led the way,
To a field of carrots that made me sway.

A rabbit in glasses read me the news,
While dress shoes danced, could I refuse?
A beard of lettuce tickled my chin,
In this wacky world, I can't help but grin.

Clouds wore polka dots, blue and pink,
A sight so absurd, made me rethink.
What's clarity, really, in a whirl?
Sometimes the nonsense makes the world swirl.

So wade through the fog, laugh at the sight,
The absurdity dances, day turns to night.
When clarity seeks, the oddball prevails,
In a life full of giggles, the laughter sails.

The Hidden Logic of the Bizarre

Cows wearing sunglasses, it's quite the view,
Discussing the weather—who knew they knew?
While chickens played chess on a checkered mat,
The farmer just sighed, what's up with that?

A vegetable band played on the street,
A cucumber's solo was oddly sweet.
The carrots kept time with their leafy hands,
In a world like this, who makes the plans?

Toast with a mustache commanded respect,
While spaghetti spoke of the love it could wreck.
Every twist of fate led to a cheer,
In this odd ballet, all were near.

So let's toast to the strange and absurd,
Life's little quirks are meant to be heard.
When logic gets tangled in a goofy dance,
Just laugh along and give it a chance.

Unwoven Dreams

Life's a puzzle with missing pieces,
Jigsaw joy, but someone sneezes.
Cats wear hats and dogs dance too,
While the toaster's plotting, it's plotting who?

Spaghetti's tangled on a sunny day,
And socks play hide-and-seek, oh yay!
The sun wears shades, the moon plays drums,
And we all believe in invisible thumbs.

Upside-down smiles with sideways frowns,
Clowns in my cereal, wearing small crowns.
Fish ride bicycles down the street,
While gravity forgets its job, quite neat!

So let's toast to life, in all its quirky thrill,
With dancing pancakes and laughter to spill.
Unraveled, we bubble, in unpredictable cheer,
Laughing at chaos, as if it were clear.

The Echoing Void

In a world where silence hums,
Cactus friends shake hands with drums.
A penguin waltzes on a grassy knoll,
While spaghetti monsters troll the shoal.

Paper boats sail on cups of tea,
With squirrels as crew, can't you see?
Buffaloes wearing tutus prance about,
And logic's a jester, there's no doubt!

Clouds whisper secrets, but they're all a tease,
While fish wear glasses, just to appease.
Time forgot its watch—what a mess!
But laughter reigns in this crazy excess!

Crayons converse in nonsensical phrases,
While zebras throw cakes at lions in mazes.
In this echoing void, humor's the lore,
Where nonsense enchants us and less is more.

A Journey Through the Unfathomable

Take a ride on a turtle's back,
Through rain made of jelly, on a zigzag track.
Kangaroos giggle at the moonlit sight,
While penguins hold court, ruling the night.

A train made of pancakes rolls on by,
With syrupy clouds dotted in the sky.
Monkeys on stilts chat with cool breeze,
In a wacky world that aims to please.

The compass spins tales of where to go,
But gumball trees just steal the show.
Maps lead to places that never were planned,
And laughter erupts when you take the stand.

So journey we must, through this fanciful space,
Where nonsense runs wild, and we find our place.
As gloves replace hats and dance the cha-cha,
In an unfathomable tale, oh là là!

Raindrops on a Foggy Day

Raindrops giggle on umbrellas bright,
As ducks debate who'll win the flight.
Fog wears a blanket, cozy and round,
While trees gossip without making a sound.

Sidewalks turn into slippery slides,
Where hedgehogs and turtles share wild rides.
Puddles reflect a carnival scene,
With rainbow balloons and a spray of green.

Clouds float by wearing polka-dot ties,
As camels do ballet, to everyone's surprise.
A sunbeam whispers, "I'm just passing through,"
Making the rainbows play peekaboo.

So here's to those foggy, rainy days,
Where giggles and mischief lead all the ways.
In a world quite silly but oh so nice,
We dance through the drops, not thinking twice.

Fragments of a Fractured Dream

A pickle in a shoe was found,
One sock's missing, what a sound.
The cat's in charge, it seems quite clear,
As it gives me that judgmental sneer.

The toast is burnt, the coffee cold,
A tale of failures, yet to be told.
I tried to dance, but tripped on air,
Life's a circus, and I'm the bear.

A puzzle piece from a different set,
The more I try, the more I fret.
A funny hat, a shoe with laces,
In this wacky world, I see strange faces.

Yet laughter bubbles in the fray,
I stumble forth, a clumsy ballet.
With every hiccup, a grin spreads wide,
Embracing chaos, I'm along for the ride.

Between Doubt and Dissonance

A frog in a wig, what a sight,
It croaks in style, oh what a fright.
The sun's a lemon, the moon's a lime,
All tastes so sour, yet I'm feeling fine.

The clock's hands dance but stand so still,
The cat's been learning to write its will.
Pancakes fly, and syrup's a bird,
In a world so silly, I'm not unheard.

A puzzle unsolved, but let's have fun,
Jigsaw pieces that don't weigh a ton.
A mismatched sock, a slip on ice,
I twirl and tumble, oh, isn't it nice?

Between the giggles and silly strife,
I find the path, this joyful life.
Each stumble leads to laughter's embrace,
In this wild dance, I've found my place.

Echoes of Uncertainty

A spoon that sings, a fork that prances,
Kitchen utensils holding strange glances.
The fridge is plotting with a lime,
Conspiring against the sands of time.

My thoughts take flight, like birds in spring,
They chirp and flutter, yet do not cling.
The garden gnomes, they chuckle and tease,
Life's riddles make me weak in the knees.

Lost in a maze of mismatched keys,
Trying to leave but caught in the breeze.
A dance with the vacuum, it pulls me tight,
In this chaos, I embrace the night.

Though echoes swirl, I laugh and spin,
Trying to find the joy within.
Wear mismatched shoes, and with a grin,
I'll tackle the oddities, let the fun begin.

Threads of a Tangled Reality

A yarn ball rolled beneath the bed,
Tangled tales spun in my head.
Each knot a story, absurd but bright,
In this fabric of life, I find delight.

A llama in sunglasses walks the street,
It struts with flair, and can't be beat.
Puns and quirks dance in my mind,
In this wacky world, joy's what I find.

The kettle whistles a tune off-key,
It's anthem for the bumblebee.
A banana peel, my trusted friend,
Makes life's little bumps feel like a trend.

With laughter, I succeed in the chase,
Embracing the madness with a smile on my face.
For in every twist, a spark shines through,
This tangled reality holds wonders anew.

Wonders of the Uncanny

Socks miss their match, they dance alone,
A cat wears a hat, thinks he's from Rome.
The toaster pops jokes, it's baking a pun,
A world full of quirks, oh, isn't it fun?

Chickens in heels strut down the street,
Waving at cars with a cluck and a beat.
A fridge sings at night, a balmy duet,
In the realm of the odd, there's no need to fret.

Fish wear tuxedos, they swim with such flair,
While clocks run in circles, and time's in mid-air.
Umbrellas get soggy from giggling too loud,
In this nonsense parade, laughter's allowed!

A keyboard has dreams of being a band,
While teacups gossip, oh so very grand.
Life's silly absurdities, we cheerfully hold,
In the chaos of charm, we're joyfully bold.

The Labyrinth Inside

I entered my head with a map made of cheese,
Found a door labeled 'Don't' that creaked with a tease.
A maze of bad puns and odd-shaped balloons,
Where the clocks tick backwards, and dance with
raccoons.

The floor is all jelly, and what do I see?
A sofa that bubbles, just like my cup of tea.
In corners of nonsense, I stumble and trip,
Over thoughts in a pickle, that just can't get a grip.

A mirror reflects my left sock with a frown,
It says life's a circus and I'm wearing a crown.
I wander through laughter, the quirks all around,
In this wacky old labyrinth, fun can be found.

The walls are all chatter, they gossip and tease,
While elephants tap dance and monkeys say please.
Getting lost in the laughter, a treasure to find,
In the puzzle of nonsense, I'm joyfully blind.

Emotions in a Tangled Web

I woke up feeling like a spaghetti noodle,
Twisted and tangled in my own little poodle.
Face like a pancake, oh who made this mess?
A swarm of emotions, I take a wild guess!

Happiness hops on a trampoline high,
While sadness throws temper tantrums by and by.
Anger's a dragon, it roars with a grin,
And joy's in a bubble, bursting within!

Confusion wears glasses, squinting at me,
Says, "Life's just a game, come roll with glee!"
Frustration's a snail moving slowly, it's clear,
But laughter's the rocket that blasts into cheer!

Each feeling a puppet, they dance in my chest,
A circus of chaos, a merry old jest.
In this tangled web, oh what a delight,
Even messy emotions can turn into flight!

A Question Mark in the Void

I found a big question mark floating by,
Winked at a cloud, said, 'What's up, oh my?'
The stars giggled softly, in lights they confound,
In this void of confusion, joy can be found.

A turtle on roller skates zoomed past my nose,
With a wink and a chuckle, a friend who just knows.
The moon plays peek-a-boo, hiding her face,
In a cosmic game of hide-and-seek space.

Balloons drift aimlessly, lost in their quest,
While the sun juggles planets, a cosmic jest.
Gravity's whimsy takes laughter in stride,
As questions and giggles, in silence, abide.

So here in this question, I twirl and I sway,
Life's riddle's a puzzle, come laugh it away!
With whimsy and wonder, we dance through the night,
In the question-filled void, everything feels right!

The Weight of Unasked Questions

Why does my sock vanish in the wash?
Did it join a sock party, wild and posh?
Are they dancing in the dryer's hot embrace?
I just want a pair, not a sockless chase.

Why do ducks cross roads in such a hurry?
Is there a sale on breadcrumbs? Oh, how they scurry!
They waddle with purpose, but I just can't see,
What secret awaits them, hidden from me?

Is that a catnip dealer I spy on the street?
Elderly cats take the bait, oh what a feat!
They strut like mobsters, with swagger and flair,
Maybe the cats know, but they never share.

Why is it I trip over air when I'm bold?
I leap like a gazelle, but alas, I am sold
To gravity's whims, a slapstick defeat,
I laugh at the ground, as it welcomes my feet.

Paper Boats on Stormy Seas

I made a paper boat to sail on a whim,
It's now on a journey quite bold and grim.
As waves start to toss it, I shout, "Don't give in!"
But it's busy debating if it's a fin.

Why do I always lose my keys at the start?
They wander like artists with a curious heart.
They play hide and seek, just to mess with my head,
While I'm late for a meeting, wishing instead.

A toaster explodes and up flies my bread,
It pirouettes like a dancer, full speed ahead.
So I munch on crumbs while I ponder the night,
Why do appliances send my toast to flight?

When life throws you curveballs, just laugh and relax,
Like playing charades with an owl and some snacks.
We'll float like those boats in uncertain delight,
And embrace all the chaos, our uncharted flight.

Navigating the Enigma

Why is the number nine so hard to define?
It's just sitting there, acting all benign.
Does it want to be ten or just hang on the line?
A number so quirky, it's truly divine!

I went to the store for some milk and a snack,
Found a parade of llamas, all dressed in black.
They rolled through the aisles with a rhythmic chant,
I stood there confused; should I cry or just dance?

Why do we ponder the mysteries of socks?
With patterns and colors like playful blocks.
As if each lost wonder holds secrets untold,
Dear sock revolution, you're so brave and bold!

At parties, I giggle at cats in top hats,
With monocles perched, they're the preppiest brats.
They sip on some tea, while I trip on my feet,
In a world that confuses, they follow the beat.

Silence in the Clamor

In a coffee shop bustling, I sip from my cup,
While a dog on the counter thinks he's savvy and up.
His bark is a symphony, rich and profound,
Yet in the oversized latte, my thoughts get drowned.

Why does my phone buzz at the worst possible time?
With messages far off, and each one a crime.
A cat in pajamas is posting a meme,
While I'm in a meeting, lost in the stream.

Is that a giraffe poking its head through the door?
My mind might be playing tricks, yet I want more!
I giggle, then blink, and I stare with dismay,
Wishing for lessons on the art of ballet.

Life's tangled like yarn in an attic so drear,
But I smile at the weirdness, knowing I'm here.
Through laughter and chaos, I'll find my own beat,
In silence, I revel, as life feels complete.

The Puzzle of Unraveled Threads

The socks are missing, where'd they go?
I trip on shoelaces, and then I show.
Instructions unclear, I still can't see,
A jigsaw mind, but missing a piece.

Cereal for dinner, pancakes at noon,
The cat is my therapist, sings me a tune.
The clock is spinning, it's lost its way,
I'll just wear my shirt inside out today.

The fridge is empty, guess I'll just snack,
Life's like a train that's off its track.
Laughter echoes in this tricky maze,
Finding my way through the silly haze.

Each day a riddle, but I do my best,
With giggles and chuckles, I pass the test.
In this wacky world, I'll still pretend,
To dance with the chaos, my funny friend.

Whispers of the Confused Heart

My heart is a GPS, lost in the woods,
It recalculates paths, misunderstood.
Love signs are crooked, colors don't match,
I'm walking in circles, yet feel the catch.

Messages tangled like spaghetti on plates,
I swipe left on love but still contemplate.
Confetti of feelings, just scattered about,
Each heartbeat a whisper, creating a doubt.

Do I cherish the goals? Or delight in the mess?
Am I up for a game or just feeling the stress?
My compass spins wildly, a real comedy,
A heart full of giggles in sweet disarray.

So let's play this game, with feeling and jest,
In this wild confusion, I'll rise with zest.
Each twist adds a smile, a story to tell,
In the whispers of chaos, I'm raving well.

Dancing in the Shadows of Doubt

I twirl with uncertainty, a wobbly dance,
With my own two left feet, I'll take a chance.
The music is quirky, the rhythm's askew,
But watch me create a thrill out of blue.

Each step's a riddle, a balance to find,
I shuffle and trip, but I'm feeling so kind.
The doubt's my partner, always on cue,
With laughter and giggles, we'll stumble right through.

Fears whisper gently, a challenging tune,
Yet here come my friends, and we'll all swoon.
We spin 'round in circles, embracing the fun,
Life's like a dance and we're never quite done.

So swing with me wildly, don't follow the plan,
Let's laugh while we wobble, just take my hand.
In shadows of doubt, we'll find our delight,
As we dance through confusion, we'll shine so bright.

Fragments of a Broken Compass

My compass is cracked, its needle spins free,
Pointing to deserts when I need the sea.
Maps made of paper, they're all upside-down,
I'm lost but I'm giggling, not wearing a frown.

I asked for directions, a squirrel just stared,
I'm searching for signs, yet no one has cared.
The trees are my guides, but they won't agree,
Tree-versations lead to a whimsical spree.

Tangled in yarn and shades of the day,
Leading me bubbling in a curious way.
Lost in the forest, what a wild quest!
Each turn is a chuckle, a comedic jest.

So here's to the journey where nothing is clear,
With laughter as fuel, there's nothing to fear.
A broken compass? I'll call it my map,
In this treasure of chaos, I'll take a long nap.

Chaotic Tides

Socks in the fridge, what a fun sight,
A frog on the sidewalk, takes flight.
Pancakes for dinner, why not, I say,
My cat thinks it's Tuesday, and it's Saturday.

Washing my keys, what a strange chore,
Found a sandwich I made, maybe a score?
Dance with a broom, so wild and free,
Even my goldfish laughed at me.

When coffee spills look like art so grand,
I take it as fate, ain't life just planned?
A pizza arrives, but it's upside down,
In this crazy circus, who wears the crown?

Mirrors talk back, I swear it's a trick,
Or maybe it's just that I need a quick flick.
Holding a book, I read with a grin,
Did I just hear that? You're not tuning in?

Laughter in the Abyss

A parrot speaks Spanish, oh what a twist,
I asked for advice, now I'm on the list.
My coffee is cold, a bitter surprise,
But it laughs at my sleepy, half-opened eyes.

Walking through mud, my shoes are now thick,
The world spins in circles, oh what a quick trick!
Balloons float by like they're in a race,
With my cereal dancing all over the place.

I tried to cook dinner, the smoke alarm sings,
The dog steals my dinner, and I try to ring.
But laughter erupts, like a crack in a tune,
Who knew chaos would dance to this tune?

With each silly moment, the puzzle's less clear,
But in every blunder, I find it sincere.
So here's to the whimsy, the giggles and glee,
Embrace the madness; just let it be free!

Unscripted Moments

A shoe on my head, how did it get there?
My plans for today went up in the air.
The toast popped up with a mighty boom,
Like life was just waiting to bring in the gloom.

Dropping my phone, oh, it bounces like glee,
Trying to capture moments, they flee from me.
A blindfolded dance on an invisible floor,
Life's just a party, but I'm not sure what for.

Unexpected phone calls, from people named Fred,
Staring at my ceiling, it's thoughts that I dread.
But I'll keep on spinning this riddle I face,
Finding the laughter in this wacky place.

So cheers to the moments that make us feel bold,
The quirks and the chaos, life's comic gold.
Let's tiptoe through laughter, let's playfully sing,
In a world where nobody knows anything!

The Weight of Unmeasured Thoughts

Moonlight on toast, what a curious meal,
Pondering whether my dishes can feel.
Lights flicker like stars, but I'm in my room,
With a cat named Whiskers, who's plotting my doom.

Juggling my keys while I search for my hat,
The fridge sings a tune, like a wayward cat.
I spilled spaghetti in a dance with my chair,
Now I'm the chef with a stylish flair.

Counting the clouds, but they're missing in action,
I trip over shadows, a comedic distraction.
The sun shines bright, yet my socks are both black,
Each wrinkle a story, none I could track.

Chasing my thoughts like a squirrel on a spree,
Where logic and reason both ran up a tree.
It's a carnival ride in this mind of delight,
With laughter as ballast, let's take off in flight!

Sifting Through Sandcastles of Thought

In a beach of dreams, I build and play,
But the tide rolls in, takes my thoughts away.
A bucket of wishes, a shovel of hopes,
I laugh at the waves, dodging slippery slopes.

Sandcastles crumble, but I still insist,
To mold new ideas with a flick of my wrist.
Each grain a memory that slips through my hands,
As I dance with the ocean, drawing in silly plans.

The seagulls above seem to mimic my plight,
They squawk and they dive, oh what a sight!
But I'm here with my pail, not a care in the world,
As my castle of nonsense continues to swirl.

So I'll scoop up the laughs, the giggles, the cheer,
In this sandy retreat, there's nothing to fear.
For in every confusion, I find a strange bliss,
In this wacky parade, I simply can't miss.

The Weight of Invisible Burdens

I walk through the day with a smile on my face,
But my backpack is filled with an unfunny space.
Invisible weights that nobody sees,
Like carrying kittens that scratch at my knees.

Each step is a dance with the wobbly ground,
My feet feel so heavy, but I'm spinning around.
I laugh at the thought of my friends on the run,
Chasing the breeze, but I'm just having fun.

They say, 'Drop your burdens,' as I wave goodbye,
But I'll juggle these puppies until I can fly.
With each little giggle, I lighten my load,
Playing hopscotch with problems, still on the road.

So here's to the laugh, the joy, and the weight,
For life's a grand circus, on a slippery crate.
And while it may seem I'm caught in the fray,
I'm a clown in this carnival, come what may!

Shattered Whispers

In a room full of echoes, I search for a word,
But the whispers are scattered, absurdly unheard.
I trip on confusion, it's a dance of the mind,
With a jigsaw of nonsense, interwoven, unkind.

Each thought is a puzzle, the pieces all fly,
I reached for a memory, it waved me goodbye.
The jokes that I tell lose their punch in the air,
As I gather my giggles like stray socks from a chair.

But laughter emerges from shadows and cracks,
Those shattered old whispers bring hearty good snacks.
I'll treasure each chuckle, each grin that I find,
In this kaleidoscope chaos, beautifully blind.

So here's to the breaks, the cracks, and the tears,
For humor survives through all of our fears.
And while swift is the breeze, and thoughts twist about,
I'll gather the laughter, and shatter the doubt!

The Puzzle Within Chaos

Jigsaw pieces scatter across my cluttered brain,
Each one a connection that dances in vain.
I try to fit shapes where they clearly don't go,
But the picture of chaos puts on quite a show.

With corners of laughter and edges of glee,
I chase after puzzles both wild and free.
The missing piece giggles, it runs in a race,
As I push and I shove in this whimsical space.

I twist and I turn, but it simply won't slot,
It's a riddle of riddles, a whimsical plot.
Yet in this confusion, I find a delight,
Each moment of chaos turns laughter to flight.

So let's celebrate jumble, embrace the unknown,
For the puzzle of madness is where love is shown.
With each silly piece that falls out of the sky,
I'll laugh with the chaos as time flutters by.

Balance on the Edge of Reason

I walked a tightrope made of cheese,
Fell into laughter with the bees.
Balancing thoughts, a wobbly dance,
Life's a riddle in a puzzling trance.

Twirling in circles like a top,
Waiting for the giggles to drop.
Clocks melt like ice on a sunny day,
Is it Tuesday or bake-a-cake day?

My shoes are mismatched, which is just fine,
Wearing polka dots in perfect line.
A cat gives sage advice on hot toast,
In this circus, I'm the silly host.

So let's all laugh as we spin and twirl,
Life's a magnificent, wobbly whirl.
We'll juggle our thoughts under a blue sky,
Hoping to land (or not!) on a pie.

Poetry of the Untold Journey

Off to the store with no list in hand,
Thought I'd find jelly, but got a band.
Hitchhiked with a penguin; he wore a hat,
Together we giggled; imagine that!

I tried to sail with a spoon and a fork,
But drifted along on the honking stork.
A llama gave directions, quite absurd,
Said, 'Just keep walking; you'll feel stirred.'

In a world where socks seem to vanish,
I'm searching for logic; oh, how I famish!
But finding a bear that can dance in tune,
Makes up for the fact that I lost my shoe.

Every wrong turn feels like a prize,
In this strange tale beneath sunset skies.
With laundry on my mind and spaghetti dreams,
Life's a comedy bursting at the seams.

An Orchid in a Storm

Oh, an orchid bloomed in the wildest storm,
Wearing a tutu, it felt quite warm.
Raindrops were dancing, tap-tap-tap,
While I lost my hat in a tornado flap.

Trees were like dancers, waving with glee,
Searching for snacks in the old apple tree.
Thunder was laughing, what a silly sound,
As I twirled in my raincoat round and round.

Horses on clouds sipped tea with delight,
Under umbrellas that took off in flight.
I asked the moon for a riddle or two,
But she just winked and gave me a clue.

So let the petals whirl in the breeze,
With giggles and snorts, I'll do as I please.
Through storms and through laughter, I'll take my stand,
Finding joy in chaos, isn't life grand?

Echoes from a Disoriented Soul

I lost my thoughts in a swirling bowl,
Chasing after whispers like a lost soul.
Banana peels danced on the kitchen floor,
While my cat debated with a green door.

Echoes of laughter kick up like dust,
In a world where logic has simply rust.
I asked a frog for some wise advice,
But he just croaked and said, 'Try some rice!'

Dreams take flight on spaghetti wings,
As time juggles silly, nonsensical things.
I painted my walls with invisible ink,
And discovered they blink when I start to think!

In the chaos of socks flying high,
I giggle and dance; oh, my, oh my!
With echoes of whimsy bouncing around,
I find all my joy in the upside-down.

Threads of a Tattered Existence

In a world that spins like a top,
I lost my socks, they just won't stop.
The dog wears shoes, the cat wears a hat,
While I'm confused, just look at that!

Chasing my dreams, they run away fast,
I take two steps, then fall on my... past.
Dancing with ghosts on a breakfast plate,
Who knew pancakes could synthesise fate?

Juggling lemons with my eyes shut tight,
Why do pickles glow in the moonlight?
The toaster sings when it's feeling bold,
A symphony of nonsense, behold!

Yet through the muddle, I find a grin,
Life's silly riddle, let the fun begin.
With tangled threads, I weave my song,
In this tapestry weird, I feel I belong.

Kaleidoscope of Confusion

My socks are mates with a can of beans,
They dance together in my daydream scenes.
The toaster sparks, it wishes to fly,
While I'm convinced that rain loves to sigh.

I asked a fish if it could skydive,
It flipped its tail as if to connive.
The clock (it's a rebel!) ticks out of time,
Inventive chaos, like nursery rhyme.

Chickens in scarves celebrate at noon,
While shadows waltz with the light of the moon.
Pineapple pizzas plot to take a stand,
In a world where oddities are so grand.

So I smile at life's absurd parade,
With every twist, let my doubts fade.
In this funhouse mirror of life today,
Who knew confusion could brighten the way?

Portrait of a Clouded Soul

I spilled my coffee on a dream today,
It brewed a storm, like clouds in May.
The moon's on vacation, and stars got lost,
In the whirlwind of thoughts, what a cost!

My shoes have stories they refuse to share,
They dance on the table without a care.
A sandwich chases me in a playful trance,
"What's the rush?" it asks, "Let's have a dance!"

Jellybeans fight, while the cake starts to sing,
A ruckus of laughter, what chaos they bring.
The bananas debate if they should be cream,
In my little world, nothing's as it seems.

Yet I chuckle at this painted facade,
Life's rainbow mess is a quirky charade.
In the shadows, I twirl with a grin so wide,
For in cloudy confusion, I'll joyfully abide!

The Riddle of Fleeting Time

A tick-tock whispers secrets of old,
While I ponder mysteries, daring and bold.
The cookies argue over who takes the prize,
Winners get milk, but it's all a surprise!

My watch decided it's a stand-up clown,
It laughs at the minutes that tumble down.
A squirrel stole time—no one saw it go,
And here I am, just riding the flow.

The walls have ears, they chat like folks,
Sharing their wisdom through laughter and jokes.
Life plays charades with a wink and a nudge,
And goofy antics always make me judge.

So I wander through riddles all wrapped in fun,
In a world so silly, my heart weighs a ton.
Every tick-tock is a dance out of line,
In this puzzling puzzle, I'm glad to dine!

The Color of Unanswered Prayers

In a world where socks go missing,
My keys decide to play hide and seek.
The cat tells jokes that I'm dismissing,
While the toaster's mocking my brunch technique.

Rain dances on my window's edge,
The umbrella's lost its sense of poise.
Coffee spills like my life's alleged pledge,
I laugh at the mess, oh what a noise!

Jellybeans sing from the candy jar,
Demanding my attention with a smile.
Spaghetti noodles look like a bizarre,
A noodle's life can stretch a mile.

In this circus where questions roam,
A rubber chicken is my best friend.
Clowns juggle dreams of a far-off home,
In laughter's arms, I find the blend.

An Odyssey of the Unconscious

My brain's a train with no set track,
The conductor's on break, sipping tea.
Thoughts collide like an asteroids' pack,
While I wonder why I can't find my keys.

A sock puppet's wisdom, oddly profound,
Guides me through this carnival of quirks.
I dance with the logic that spins 'round and 'round,
With gummy bears writing all of my works.

The calendar's mixed up all the days,
Tomorrow's gone. Where'd it go?
I'm caught in a loop of oddball displays,
Chasing my tail in a comedic show.

In the maze of thoughts that twist and turn,
A rubber band ball tells tales with flair.
In the chaos, there's fun that I earn,
Life's a riddle, but I simply don't care.

The Canvas of Confusion

They say the grass is always greener,
But mine's a patchwork of polka dots.
Each brush stroke's a puzzling demeanor,
While my lunch decides to join the knots.

Pigs paint rainbows on cloudy days,
As I try to solve a jigsaw fate.
Cucumbers wear hats in quirky ways,
And jam spreads rumors about my plate.

A monster lurks in my fridge's depths,
It giggles at expired buckets of cheese.
While I ponder all these odd concepts,
The blender just winks, ready to tease.

Each hiccup's an artist with vivid strokes,
Splatters of laughter, splashes of blues.
For the whole world's a canvas of jokes,
A masterpiece brewed from whimsical views.

Silence in the Midst of Noise

In loudest rooms, my thoughts take flight,
An orchestra of chaos in my mind.
A washing machine startles in the night,
While the blender's lost its vegan grind.

Chickens in bow ties dance on the floor,
Singing opera as I try to think.
With every honk, and every uproar,
Fruits whisper secrets in culinary ink.

The world spins tales, obnoxiously grand,
Like squirrels plotting mischief on a spree.
Yet in the din, I find a band,
Of laughing echoes playing with glee.

In this chaos, I embrace the cheer,
As breadcrumbs lead me astray, no doubt.
Amidst the noise, my muse appears,
Crafting oddities that I can't live without.

The Labyrinth of Lost Reason

In a maze of socks and missing shoes,
I search for answers, yet confuse.
The cat's judging me, perched on high,
While I wonder why my toast can't fly.

Pants inside out, and peanut butter hair,
Sipping tea with a rubber bear.
The clock ticks backward, time's a jest,
But I giggle on, just like the rest.

Chasing thoughts like flies in June,
My mind's a circus, an absurd tune.
Each twist and turn leads to strange sights,
Like broccoli wearing tiny tights.

Still, I wander, no road map near,
And dance with shadows, full of cheer.
What's lost in sense is found in fun,
In this twisted game, we all have won.

Dissonant Chords

I played a note on the piano grand,
But it turned out to be a rubber band.
The dog joined in with a bark and a howl,
Making music that made the fish scowl.

Melodies jumbled in a tangled mess,
Accordion dreams in a polka dress.
My conductor's wand is a broomstick bright,
Leading chaos into the night.

The audience laughs, they've all got a hat,
As turtles tango and squirrels chit-chat.
In the cacophony, I find my groove,
For nonsense is where the giggles move.

So let the dings and dongs resound,
In this orchestra of life, absurdly found.
For when the notes don't fit, ha ha!
We create a symphony, a quirky star.

In the Absence of Clarity

I woke up today to a fish in my shoe,
It blinked at me like it fancied a view.
The walls are whispering secrets and lies,
While my breakfast cereal dances and flies.

Chickens in coats are hosting a ball,
Underneath my desk, an octopus crawls.
The microwave is plotting with the fridge,
Panting for popcorn as they sit on the ridge.

I sip my juice, it tastes like a shoe,
Mixing flavors, purple polka dot stew.
Questions swirl in my coffee cup,
Filled with answers I can't ever sup.

Yet in this haze where sense takes a break,
Laughter erupts, for fun's the take.
In the swirl of upside-down light,
I find my joy, my heart feels right.

The Winding Path of Questions

Down the lane where odd ducks waddle,
I ponder the meaning of that strange model.
Why does the sky wear a polka dot scarf?
And why do fish schools do the math farce?

The trees gossip like they've lost their minds,
While ants hold meetings, discussing the signs.
I ask the snail, 'What's the meaning of fate?'
He shrugs and says, 'I'm just a late mate.'

Under a lamppost with a spaghetti hat,
I twirl my thoughts like a bouncy cat.
Questions tumble like balls on a hill,
Chasing each other, they refuse to be still.

With each twist on this curious road,
Laughter burgeons, lightens the load.
For every riddle with no clear reply,
Beneath the weirdness, we laugh and we fly.

The Labyrinth of Uncertainties

I wore my socks, one blue, one red,
And walked outside to clear my head.
A pigeon cooed, laughed at my plight,
As I searched for answers in the light.

I asked the wall, 'What should I do?'
It just stood there, painted in blue.
The trees whispered secrets, I couldn't have guessed,
While the sun did a jig, quite underdressed.

I tripped on my thoughts, fell flat on my face,
A tumble of logic, a humorous chase.
With giggles around, I'm a clumsy ballet,
In the maze of the day, I just sway and sway.

So if you ever feel lost in a mess,
Just laugh at the chaos, it's anyone's guess.
For the more that we ponder, the sillier it gets,
Like socks full of holes, in mismatched sets.

When Certainty Resides in Shadows

I brewed my coffee, and oh what a scene,
It splashed on the counter, a caffeinated dream.
The cat looked aghast, then licked up the floor,
It seems even felines want more and more.

Emails pile up like a tower of bricks,
And every shot fired feels like a few kicks.
'What day is it now?' I question with glee,
As my calendar mocks, 'It's still just Tuesday!'

The toast is still bread, though gloated and jammed,
While my breakfast debate with a spoon has been planned.

I argue with shadows, they dance and they sway,
Just to remind me I'm losing the day.

But in the end, as the chaos unfolds,
There's humor in every clumsy handhold.
So let out a chuckle, embrace the odd fun,
For life is a comedy, well more than a run.

Reflections of a Dizzy Mind

A mirror replied with a quirky grin,
'You're looking quite well, for someone in spin!'
With toothpaste on lips and plans upside down,
I waltzed into traffic, wearing my frown.

The bus honked its horn, a blast from the past,
As I tried to recall which way I was cast.
Each step a question, each turn a jest,
Like a juggler with balls that won't let him rest.

I tripped on my thoughts, in a loop-de-loop race,
With a brain made of jelly, oh what a place!
The sun gave a wink, clouds rolled with delight,
As I danced with confusion, all day and all night.

In the end, in the fun, there's a lesson to find,
Life's a wild ride, pulls at the mind.
So let's spin with the whirl, in hugs and in laughs,
For laughter's the compass on chaotic paths.

The Enigma in Everyday Moments

I opened the fridge, what did I behold?
A jar full of pickles, neglected and cold.
'Are you wise?' I asked, as it stared back at me,
In a pickle of thoughts, what could life be?

The toaster just hummed, what wisdom it keeps,
While the dirty old dishes conspired in heaps.
I wondered aloud, 'Where's my other shoe?'
Then I found that it also felt quite askew.

The leaves in the garden whispered to me,
'Embrace the bizarre, just let it all be.'
So I danced with the daisies, twirled with a bee,
While life giggled softly, playing tricks on me.

In corners we find the humor we seek,
In shadows and sunlight, both curious and meek.
So here's to the moments that wobble and weave,
For in the grand puzzle, we learn to believe.

Dreams Unhinged by Reality

Chasing unicorns through thick fog,
Sipping tea with a purple dog.
Giraffes in hats dance in my dreams,
While reality bursts at the seams.

Rainy days bring puddles of pie,
As time flies by like a rubber fly.
Counting clouds that wear polka dots,
In a world where confusion rots.

The toaster sings tunes of regret,
While socks and shoes play charades, you bet!
A cat gives lectures on quantum leaps,
And I just wonder where sanity sleeps.

So let's frolic in a field of cheese,
With dancing spoons that aim to please.
Who needs sense when nonsense is grand?
Join the party; life's out of hand!

The Paradox of Glances Lost

Lost my keys in a bowl of soup,
Swam with fish in an upside-down loop.
The clock strikes cheese instead of chime,
Every second like a pickle in rhyme.

Winking at shadows in the midnight sun,
Laughing at bricks on the run for fun.
A parade of ants carried the moon,
While giggling stars hummed a funky tune.

Jumbled thoughts in a blender spin,
Pouring ideas like glitter on kin.
I tried to find sense in my mismatched socks,
But all they did was dance in flocks.

So here I stand, unclear yet bold,
With tales of bizarre yet never old.
Each glance a riddle, each laugh a prize,
In this topsy-turvy world, I rise!

In Search of Meaning Amongst the Clutter

Searching for meaning in a stack of chips,
Chasing after life's funny little quips.
Lost a sandwich in a mountain of socks,
And time plays hopscotch with a box of rocks.

Pancakes rain down in puzzling form,
As I twirl with joy in a thunderstorm.
A rubber duck sings opera so grand,
While the cat takes charge of the marching band.

To find some logic in jellybeans,
Or decipher a world filled with silly scenes.
Every cluttered thought in a tangle spins,
Like a hamster in dreams, oh where to begin?

So let's throw confetti in a hurricane,
And dance through the chaos, ignoring the pain.
For in this clutter, we might find glee,
In the mess of life, just you and me!

Echoes of Unanswerable Questions

Why does a donut have a hole, you see?
And who invented the letter 'Q'?
The echoes of queries bounce off the wall,
As waffles wear hats, preparing for fall.

Riding a turtle with a wheeze and a whee,
Searching for answers in a glass of tea.
A llama debates with a wise old owl,
While snickering teapots giggle and scowl.

Will never-ending what-ifs dance on the breeze?
Or will cupcakes solve mysteries with ease?
In a circus of thoughts, I juggle and spin,
And wonder why life's a pancake with skin.

So let's raise a toast with confounding cheer,
To the questions that linger, year after year.
In the land of the zany, no answers are wrong,
Just echoes of nonsense, our eternal song!

www.ingramcontent.com/pod-product-compliance
Ingram Content Group UK Ltd.
Pitfield, Milton Keynes, MK11 3LW, UK
UKHW010437170125
4146UKWH00047B/197

9 781805 661566